ALL
IN
THE
WILD

Calling

JASON LEO BANTLE

RESPECT NATURE RESPECT NATURE RESPECT NATURE RESPECT NATURE RESP

Jason Leo Bantle

ALL IN THE WILD CALLING - JASON LEO BANTLE
1st Edition Print
© Text copyright @ 2010 Jason Leo Bantle
© Photograph copyright @ 2010 Jason Leo Bantle

Library and Archives Canada Cataloguing in Publication

Bantle, Jason Leo, 1972-
        All in the wild : calling / Jason Leo Bantle.

Includes index.
ISBN 978-0-9783406-4-3

        1. Bantle, Jason Leo, 1972-. 2. Wildlife photography.
3. Animals--Canada--Pictorial works. I. Title.

TR647.B388 2010   779'.32092   C2010-902153-3

Design & Layout by Jason Leo Bantle & Lori Nunn
                            CRMM Services
                            nunn@agt.net

Edited by Meagan Gilmour & Lori Nunn

Printed in Canada by Friesens Corporation
                ————One Printers Way
                    Altona, Manitoba
                    R0G 0B0

Published by Jason Leo Bantle Publishing
            Box 61
            Christopher Lake, Saskatchewan
            S0J 0N0

All images in the book were photographed using
NIKON equipment and captured on FUJI film

RESPECT NATURE   RESPECT NATURE   RESPECT NATURE   RESPECT NATURE

Dedication

To all of YOU who enjoy my art and Respect Nature and to the animals that want to be famous. Thank you for helping me live and spread a passion that calls me.

Wildlife photographer Jason Leo Bantle volunteeri
on an arctic fox research project in 2009.

I believe in God, only I spell it Nature.
Frank Lloyd Wright

Photographed by Gustaf Samelius.

Table of Contents

Sections

Grey Owl came from the wilds of Canada. He lectured throughout Canada, the United States and Great Britain about the threat humans posed to wildlife. He was internationally recognized as a renowned naturalist, a gifted speaker and an author. His death in 1938 brought the truth of this man Grey Owl to light. His long-standing claim of being an Aboriginal person of Canada was fraudulent. In fact he was born in Britain, an Englishman by the name of Archibald Belaney. His life story and its meaning have survived because of his message.

"Kindness to animals is the hallmark of human advancement; when it appears nearly everything else can be taken for granted."

"Remember you belong to Nature, not it to you."

"This thing of hunting and living in the bush generally is not what it is in the books...it is not near as interesting as it seems, to be eaten up day and night by black ants, flies and mosquitoes, to get soaked with rain or burnt up with heat, to draw your own toboggan on snowshoes and to sleep out in sixty to seventy degrees below zero...A man who makes his living in the bush earns it."

"If a man believes in himself without conceit, puts everything of which he is capable into his project, and carries on in absolute sincerity of purpose, he can accomplish nearly any reasonable aim."

"...when I stood on these platforms, I did not need to think. I merely spoke of the life and animals I had known all my days. I was only the mouth, but nature was speaking."

"We need an enrichment other than material prosperity and to gain it we have only to look around at what our country has to offer."

"Why should the last of the Silent Places be destroyed ruthlessly whilst we stand by in listless apathy, without making an effort...to provide sanctuary for the Spirit of the Wild and for those of us, and they are not few, who live to commune with Him and His furred and feathered people."

Quotes by Grey Owl

Introduction

It is 11:15 PM on March 7th, 2010, and I am sitting in my car in Hudson Bay, Saskatchewan. In a few minutes I will be catching a train north to Churchill, Manitoba. When I arrive at my destination I will have to be ready to hit the ground running for I will have limited time to find and photograph the polar bear cubs that I'm hoping to see. As I sit and wait I find myself questioning, as any normal person would, what exactly I am doing by the side of the tracks at nearly midnight waiting for a train to appear! Could it be that I am having a mid-life crisis and don't realize it? I think that it's more likely that my passion drives me to do seemingly crazy things sometimes.

I am off again on another wildlife photography adventure because, quite simply, I love to be out in the wild. I live a nomadic life, often away from home, family and friends for weeks at a time. The thing is though, they will still be there when I get back. It is a gift to be able to spend so much time in the wild surrounded by all of the amazing nature that Canada has to offer. One of the things that children are often told is to find something that they are passionate about and then figure out how to make a living at it. I guess that I have done exactly that.

The lifestyle that I have chosen is far from typical, but perhaps I have always been unconventional. That said, for all its benefits, the road that I have chosen in my life can often be quite solitary. A lot of my mornings begin early, often while it is still dark outside. I get up, brush my teeth, put in my contact lenses and put on whatever clothing will be appropriate for the day outdoors. I'll grab some fruit and a couple of granola bars along with a jug of water and make numerous trips to my vehicle to load my camera gear. The constant challenge is to be ahead of the sun! I don't have a day-to-day work routine with regular morning coffee and co-workers to share last night's events with. Then again, I don't drink coffee and with the phone and internet friends are often easily accessible! The animals themselves create a different kind of social group for me and we communicate in our own ways.

Routine things like regular weekly television don't rank high on my priority list. I suppose I could get a recorder if they did! Mother Nature has some of the most fascinating and entertaining shows that I've ever seen. Even though I can be gone for long periods of time I have no regrets. Trips like this one to Churchill are such exciting opportunities. Getting to spend my time with a species as incredible as the polar bear, that's priceless!

With that said, as I sit by the tracks on this dark night I can't help but worry about what the next days will bring. Will we even find polar bears? If we do will they be cooperative subjects? Will the light be good? Will my camera equipment be up to the challenge? Will I? *WHOO, whoo!* I hear the train in the distance, I guess my questioning will have to wait. The train is a few minutes early, it is now 11:23 PM. The thirty hour train ride ahead will give me plenty of time to grapple with the mysteries of life – oh, and give me a chance to start on the introduction to All in the Wild Calling!

I'm sure that I'm not the only one who questions the choices that they've made. I find lately, however, that the voice in my head has a lot of questions! Why did I decide to become a biologist instead of a professional golfer? Why did I decide to teach instead of pursuing a life as a research biologist? Why did I decide to quit teaching to become a wildlife photographer? Why did I decide to move to northern Saskatchewan and buy a dilapidated old restaurant and renovate it into a home and art gallery? Why do I continually make the challenging choice? I suppose that it's like the song says, "...the answers my friend are blowin' in the wind."

By letting the wind blow me where it wished, I have ended up in a pretty fortunate place. The old restaurant isn't dilapidated anymore. My artistic side is fulfilled through photography. I get to share the way that I see and love nature with others, which is always exciting. Perhaps the best part of all though is that I get to be out in the wild as much as possible and it is there that I am at peace. The cold breeze on my face, or the bite of a mosquito on the back of my neck, or the smell of a forest in spring, these are the things that awaken my senses and make me feel truly alive.

To have an experience with a species other than your own, to communicate in a language that is neither theirs nor yours but one that is shared between you, can be a magical experience. I believe that the more open we are to having these types of encounters the more often they will present themselves. Being in nature helps me to remember where it is that we came from not so long ago. The luxuries that surround many of us used to be uncommon and yet in a very short span of time we have started to take our amenities for granted. Our reality is not as separate from the animals as we'd like to believe despite our place on the food chain. It is crucial to remember that we are all interconnected and the more time spent in nature the harder that fact is to ignore.

We are no different than any other living organism on the planet when it comes to our ability to adapt. Adapt and survive or don't and won't, that is the harsh reality. During a recent trip to Toronto for an art exhibition, it was interesting to observe one of the many ways that we humans have adapted to our environment. On a Friday night after the show I was taking a packed streetcar back to my hotel. I must admit this particular situation was far from comfortable for me. It was obvious that the streetcar had not been designed to carry this number of people and many of us were standing shoulder to shoulder. I thought about how back at my home a week can easily go by during the cold winter months when I won't see another human being! As I looked at the people around me though, it suddenly occurred to me that they weren't feeling nearly as uncomfortable as I was. I suppose that if you commuted this way to and from work everyday, you would simply adapt. I also thought about how much better this was for the environment by keeping so many cars off the road. Maybe my preference for being alone in the wilderness is just how I have adapted. That being said, I was happy when the streetcar finally reached my stop!

Later that night, I couldn't help but wonder if the animals in the wild feel the same way that I did while I was packed onto that streetcar. Just a century ago there were very few people living in Canada and the animals were free to roam where they wished. There have always been changes in the environment that nature has had to make adjustments for. The current changes though are occurring at such a rapid pace that it is impossible for nature to keep up. Animals often don't have the same options as we do when it comes to choosing how they want their lives to unfold. It would be reasonable to think that if the animals had their choice, things would go back to the way they were before people began to fracture the wild places.

Like the people in the streetcar, the animals in nature are being squeezed closer and closer together. The wild places are getting fewer and further between and there are people virtually everywhere. Imagine if the situation was reversed and nature was infringing on us! We would have trees popping up in the middle of our living rooms, creatures moving into our cupboards and our homes would constantly be warmer than we'd like. Thank goodness that isn't the case, but it is something to think about. Mother Nature is very good to us and accommodates us. Canada is thankfully still a place with very large natural areas that are relatively abundant with wildlife. We all need to work together so that these areas remain for the future.

As I travel down the tracks towards Churchill, I spend a lot of time staring out the window while lost in thought. At one point I spot signs in the snow of a trapper that has recently been in the forest, the tracks in the snow clearly lead to a "marten set" on a tree. These tracks represent a traditional life that was once common and ensured the survival of people in an inhospitable wilderness. Today only remnants of that life exist in Canada.

Many people would have missed these signs altogether for these are skills that I learned as a child. Much of my knowledge of wildlife and wild places was passed down to me by a trapper when I was young and from growing up on the land. This mentor taught me invaluable lessons that have been very useful in my current life as a wildlife photographer. I learned how to be a part of nature which is something that cannot be taught in a classroom setting.

For many of us a trapper's life can seem cruel. For me what's tough is a living thing dying to fill the needs of another. Living organisms die daily to fill the needs of another, this is nature! So many of us live in a way that is very detached from the truth of nature. Trappers see exactly what they are taking from the environment to provide for their own survival, does that mean their life is more in tune with nature? Perhaps neither way is right or wrong, just different. There is no doubt in my mind though, that if each of us was forced to look directly at what we are taking from nature, we would all choose to take a little less.

I am reminded of a story that I heard years ago from an elder in Churchill. The elder had grown up in the area as a trapper's daughter. She talked about how the boys and girls would be sent out in the springtime to hunt for eggs. The parents would tell the children that if there were four eggs in the nest, they could take two. If the nest had two or three eggs they could take one and if there was only a single egg they should take none. The elder laughed as she was convinced that the boys did not listen as they always came home with more eggs than the girls. She also said that one side of the lake would have fewer ducks the next year. The guidelines set by her parents were to ensure that there was a balance to how nature was being managed. By taking too many eggs, the boys not only cheated at the egg collection but cheated everyone for the future.

The developed world today has changed from the one that the elder experienced as a child. It is very easy to disconnect our resource taking from the impact that it will have in the future. I myself am guilty of this detachment. The resources required to develop a roll of film or to fuel the train to Churchill I have little understanding of. Where the resources came from and how they will be used for my personal needs are hard for me to grasp because I didn't take the resources directly, they come to me in a roundabout way. I didn't personally take the eggs from the nest. I suppose that asking the relevant questions is the first step to getting a deeper understanding.

As I refocus on my life in this book, there is one fact that I do not question: being a wildlife photographer is my calling. I believe profoundly that it is my place in life to share my experiences in nature with others. I always say that there are animals that "want to be famous" and it's my job to facilitate that for them. I am honoured to share a part of their life with all. I am also honoured that Mother Nature cooperates with me as often as she does! Although I capture images that depict experiences that I have had, once I share them, they belong to everyone. I can share the story behind the photograph, the mood of the day, the sounds and the smells. Each person who hears the story will interpret it their own way. My story will mesh with the listener's experiences to create a unique feeling for each person.

Nature belongs to everyone, the animals and the images speak for themselves. Different images will cause different reactions in people. One person may smile at an image that will give someone else the chills. That is one of the great things about art, it is an individual experience. I often feel as though the animals are speaking for themselves through my artwork and with that they are helping me to achieve my purpose. It is a mutually beneficial arrangement!

It isn't uncommon for people to comment that I am a lucky person to have the job I have. There is no doubt that I have been extremely fortunate to have seen the moments *All in the Wild* that I've seen. When I set out on this path I could have never imagined that it would turn out the way that it has. How could I have? You simply can't predict what each day will bring when you're out in the wild. On a day in the Arctic, for instance, you may get up in the morning and secretly hope to see a pack of seventeen wolves on the tundra, but to have it actually happen? (The Matriarch, Page 153) What an incredible and unlikely day that was!

I believe however that although these experiences are unlikely, they aren't all purely luck. I choose to put myself in places where intimate moments with nature can happen. Then, I choose to be open to whatever unfolds. In my own way I suppose that I am *calling* to Mother Nature and then waiting for her reply. I search, I watch, I keep my eyes wide open and my other senses focused. We all have those abilities. I urge everyone to spend time in nature and you may find that you too are an extremely lucky person!

I believe that animals have a very strong sixth sense when it comes to the energy in their environments. They pick up on the most subtle cues. I have found that if I try to rush a shot or pressure an animal into doing what I want it to do, the shot often fails. I have come to believe that the animals can sense whether my intentions are good at that instant or not. Am I truly appreciating what they are giving me, absorbing the experience, or am I not? When I enter a situation I try to remain quiet and always respectful, remembering that I am a guest. When I leave a situation I always say thank you.

Respect is a vital part of being successful as a wildlife photographer. A mutual respect between me and my subject must be present for the situation to be safe and for the shot to work out. Imagine how foreign it must

have been for a spirit bear on a remote island off the British Columbia coast to walk out of the rainforest and see three people sitting on the opposite riverbank. (Legend of the Rainforest, Page 79) We were likely the first humans that this bear had ever encountered. The bear judged the situation and read our cues and decided that we presented no threat. We were only there to watch him, photograph him, and share his life for a brief time. He granted us time to share in his life as he went about his day fishing in the river. To be accepted in that way is an indescribable feeling.

It is my honour to share my experiences captured on film, my passion and my love of nature with everyone. I am fortunate to get to share the collection of images found in All in the Wild Calling with its readers. What can you expect as the reader of this book? Firstly, the majority of the images between the covers have never been released in book format before. Along with the images are the stories of how they were captured. Every image contained in this book was captured with 35mm film. There are no digital enhancements. I am still a film photographer, despite a few of the technological disadvantages, because it is a medium that I love. The mounting pressure to make the switch to digital however, may mean that this will be my last book where one hundred percent of the images are captured with film. Please enjoy the unique moments in this book that the animals have so graciously chosen to share and be *famous* for.

introduction continued on page 168...

FLYING BIRDS can be both extremely challenging and fun to photograph. It requires a combination of skill, equipment and steady movements to capture these individuals in flight. Tracking a flying bird through a viewfinder means panning along with it while it is in motion. Having a lens with a long focal length and autofocus can be helpful for capturing birds in flight. Birds have superior eyesight and are generally wary of anything that doesn't look natural to them. This means that many opportunities for bird photography occur as the subject is flying away! Although it is more difficult to focus a camera manually when the subject is moving as quickly as a flying bird, it is sometimes more accurate than relying on the camera to autofocus in time. Shutter speeds generally have to be quite fast as well, usually 1/1000th of a second or faster to freeze the motion of the bird. Shutter speeds this fast are not always possible in natural lighting conditions with film. If circumstances are not ideal then creativity can come into play and some very artistic images can be created. Quick response times are helpful when photographing flying birds.

SWIMMING BIRDS offer a completely different set of challenges when it comes to photography. Using a blind on shore and remaining completely hidden is helpful. A long lens is used to bridge the distance between the blind and the bird. Even from a blind it is important to not move the exposed camera lens too quickly as birds can easily spot the subtlest motion. Another option for photographing swimming birds is to enter their environment in a kayak. Swimming birds tend to be quite trusting of a kayak and will often allow a kayaker to approach closely. Natural balance and a steady hand are required for this type of photography. A windy day and the ensuing waves can deter these shooting excursions as tipping over with camera in hand would be detrimental to capturing a good shot. A dry bag is necessary to pack gear away when traveling to and from subjects as well. It is difficult to hold a long lens in these circumstances but usually a shorter lens is adequate because of the close proximity to the subjects. Becoming part of the environment is advantageous when photographing swimming birds.

PERCHED BIRDS generally require a lot of scouting and then an equal amount of patience to photograph. Certain bird species prefer to use familiar perches day after day. They may use the perch as a site to sing and mark their territory or perhaps to try to attract a mate. The perch may also serve as a spot to look for prey or to watch for predators entering the area. Natural blinds are useful but again it is important to not move the camera too much. Any unfamiliar movement in the area and a perched bird is likely to become a flying bird! If a bird is startled away from its perch, it is not uncommon for it to be many hours or even the next day before it feels comfortable enough to return. As a perched bird holds reasonably still, manual focus and slow shutter speeds can often be used for this type of photography. Keeping a fair amount of distance from the bird is helpful in ensuring that it doesn't get scared away so a long lens is required. Being familiar with the favourite perches in a given area is useful when photographing perched birds.

Flying, Swimming and Perched Birds

RESPECT NATURE RESPECT NATURE RESPECT NATURE RESPECT NATURE

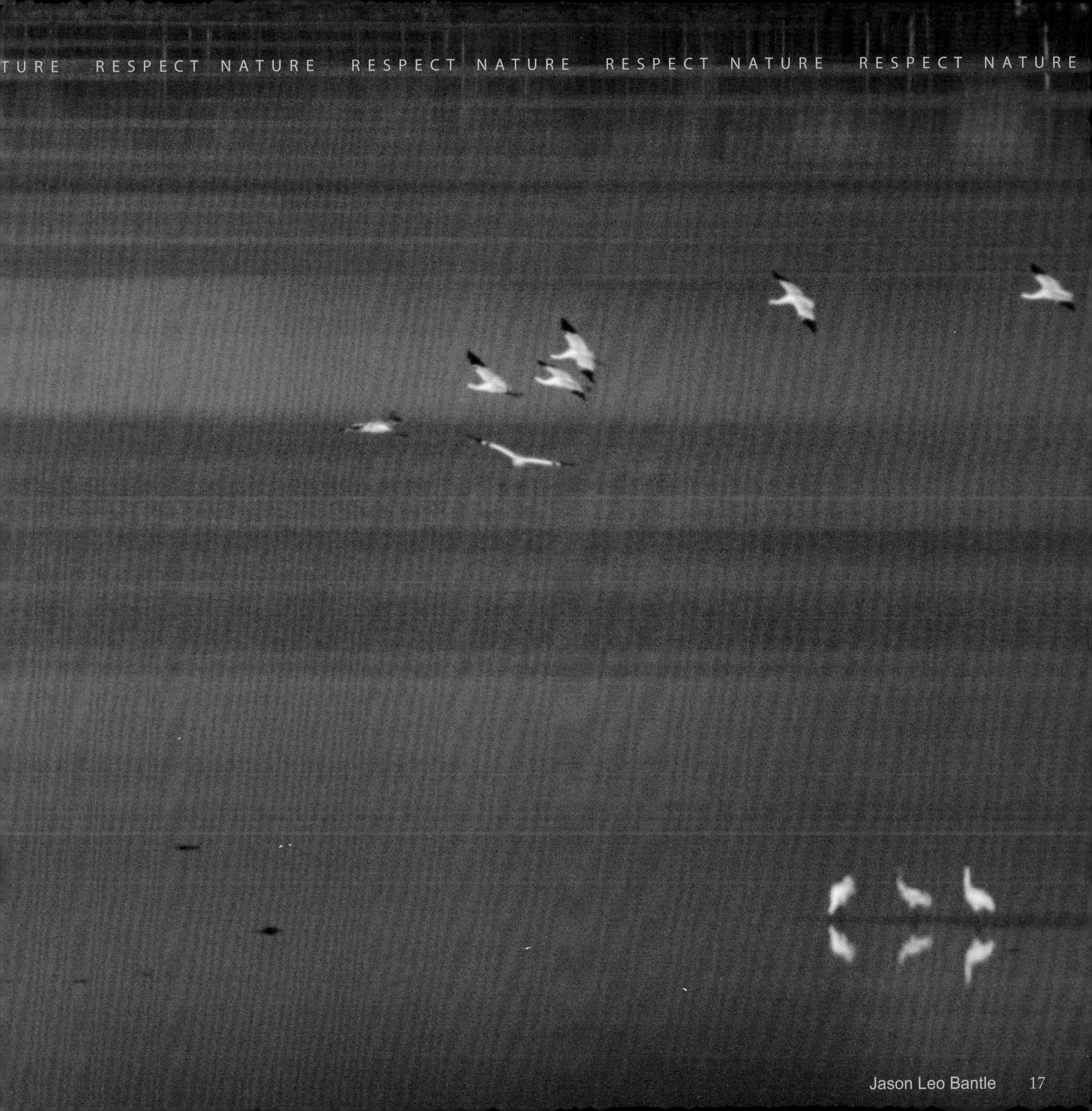
TURE RESPECT NATURE RESPECT NATURE RESPECT NATURE RESPECT NATURE

"RETURNING FOR A REST"
Cudworth, Saskatchewan
(above)

Whooping cranes are often seen near my hometown of Cudworth in the spring and fall as they follow their migratory path. They are the tallest bird in North America, standing around five feet in height, and are considered to be critically endangered. Since the late 1960s breeding efforts have been underway in an attempt to help the population recover. There has been some success with these efforts and seeing a flock such as this one is promising. I had heard that the cranes had returned to the area so I went out searching for them on several occasions. While out with my father one evening we found this group feeding in a field. As night drew nearer, three of the cranes flew off towards a nearby pond. We relocated to the pond in the hopes that the rest of the birds would soon follow. When they did I was able to capture this image as they came in to roost for the night.

A small warbler perched on an aspen branch.

"STELLAR STELLER"
Vancouver Island, British Columbia

The Steller's jay is part of the corvid family along with ravens, crows, jays, magpies, nutcrackers and a hundred or so others. They are an extremely intelligent family of birds and also tend to be quite opportunistic. This individual was foraging near a picnic area, watching for food to be dropped by tourists. He would fly off and cache the food he collected before quickly returning for more. He came quite close to me at one point as I ate, obviously looking for a handout! They are a beautiful bird and the blue of their feathers can be almost iridescent. After posing for a photograph, he moved on to try his luck with someone else.

"HOMEWARD BOUND"
Homer, Alaska

In the late 1970s, when bald eagles were on the endangered species list, a woman named Jean Keene happened to move to Homer. While working at the local fish processing plant, Jean began to feed the eagles that were in the area with the scrap and spoiled fish parts from work. There were two eagles to start, and then six, then dozens and ultimately over two hundred birds a day would congregate for feeding time. Jean fed the eagles every year from December until early spring for over three decades. At this time the eagles would be making their way up the coast of Alaska to their nesting grounds. Jean's feeding program helped to ensure that the eagles arrived in prime condition to lay their eggs and raise their young. Due in no small part to the efforts of people like Jean, who became known to all as the "Eagle Lady", bald eagle numbers are flourishing and they were removed from the endangered species list in 2007. I had the pleasure of visiting Jean's eagle sanctuary and witnessing firsthand the passion that she had for the eagles. Jean Keene passed away in 2009 at the age of eighty-five. Her sanctuary has been closed as the eagle population is now large and healthy enough to survive on its own. This image, photographed just off the Homer Spit near Jean's feeding grounds, was released and titled in her honour.

"SWIMMING LESSON"
Prince Albert National Park, Saskatchewan

From my kayak I spotted a loon on her nest. She was quite cooperative and didn't seem concerned about me in my kayak so I returned day after day to check on the nest's progress. Finally in early July I saw a chick nestled under her wing in the nest. Loons generally have one or two chicks a year and the babies are able to swim almost immediately after hatching. A couple of days later when I went back to check on the family, I found that there were indeed two chicks out for a swim with one of their parents. Swimming is tiring work for the newborns and they'll often climb onto a parent's back for a rest and to conserve energy.

What I saw from my kayak most days:
mother loon sitting on her nest.

Both parents taking the chicks for
a swimming lesson.

A loon parent teaching its
chick how to fish.

Various shots of Flare while I spent time with him.

"FLARE"
Aberdeen, Saskatchewan

Over the course of a month one winter, I spotted six different snowy owls living in the same four square mile area. They had a number of favourite perches so I set up remote cameras in an attempt to capture them perched. They tend to be quite wary birds and were having no part of the strange remote camera boxes! I changed my approach to hiding under a white snow blind in full winter gear and tracking them through my viewfinder. On an especially cold day I watched this snowy owl as it hunted a field for prey. Research has shown that in winter a snowy owl must eat the equivalent of seven to ten mice a day to remain healthy. When this owl flared as part of its approach, I was given a beautiful view of his outstretched feathers.

"COMMANDER-IN-CHIEF"
Homer, Alaska

One of the most regal sights in nature has to be the white feathering on the head of a bald eagle. This is a sign of maturity as the white feathers do not develop until a bald eagle is four or five years old. The eagles in this part of Alaska have become accustomed to human presence over the years and I was able to get quite close to this individual. He perched proudly as though he was the commander-in-chief posing for an official portrait!

The goal of life is living in agreement with Nature.
Zeno

Jason Leo Bantle 27

"INTENSE FOCUS"
Mayview, Saskatchewan

This beautiful great gray owl was in the area for about a month one year. Every morning and evening I would go out and watch as it hunted a favourite meadow. These owls stand around two and a half feet tall and can have a wingspan of up to five feet! Fine barbs on their feathers help to dampen the sound as they cut through the air, an adaptation that is very useful as they hunt for the small rodents that make up the bulk of their diet. On multiple occasions I watched this individual successfully retrieve its prey from under the snow. Although docile in temperament, the focus that this owl exhibited when hunting was incredible to witness.

"CATCH OF THE MORNING"

Prince Albert National Park, Saskatchewan

While on the northern shore of Waskesiu Lake I spotted this osprey. It was nervously perched with a small fish in its talons. Ospreys have keen eyesight and it was obviously aware that I was watching it. It is not uncommon for eagles to try to steal an osprey's catch and perhaps this individual was concerned that I was about to give chase. These large raptors are incredibly skilled at fishing and can spot their prey from up to forty feet above the water. From there they hover momentarily before plunging feet-first into the water to capture their prey. The osprey didn't want to chance losing its meal and flew off shortly after I captured this image.

"GUARDIANS OF THE RAINFOREST"
Near Stewart, British Columbia

I had been photographing grizzlies in northern British Columbia as they fed on salmon in a river. On one day trip away from grizzly bear photography I spotted these two bald eagles in an old snag. I decided to climb up a scree slope to get a better angle. As I climbed I realized just what a spectacular backdrop there was for this photograph. It was a wonderful surprise to have the waterfall in the background on a misty day to really showcase the eagles in their rainforest environment. I think that this image truly captures the essence of the British Columbia rainforest.

"FOREST INSPECTOR"
Prince Albert National Park, Saskatchewan
(right)

The pileated woodpecker is a year-round resident of Saskatchewan's boreal forest. This image was captured near Birch Bay as I witnessed this individual pecking holes in a tree to find lunch. Their distinctive drumming can often be heard as they drill into tree trunks to look for insects. About the same size as a crow, these birds are distinguished by their red crest and white lines that extend down either side of their throat. Each year pileated woodpecker pairs burrow a new hole in a tree to raise their young. Once the brood is raised the family will abandon the hole and will not use it again the following year. These abandoned holes provide future homes for many forest song birds. As such, the entire woodpecker family is important to the well-being of many other bird species.

Forest Inspector in flight.

Jason

A forest showing the negative effect that the population explosion of the pine beetle has produced.

"EVENING HOVER"
Tweedsmuir, Saskatchewan
(left)

This image was photographed right at my home near Tweedsmuir. I have a number of hummingbird feeders and typically four to six ruby-throated hummingbirds visit regularly during the summer. Besides the feeders, the hummingbirds seem to enjoy the delphiniums that bloom in my yard. This male hummingbird liked one particular bunch of flowers so much that it was not uncommon to see him chasing others from the area! Hummingbirds beat their wings around fifty times per second, making it virtually impossible to follow them with a camera lens. Instead, I chose to set my camera up in a spot that he frequented and employed the patience that is so well-known to a wildlife photographer. I was able to capture him in silhouette as he hovered in the early evening light.

"EAGLE INQUISITION"
Homer, Alaska

This curious eagle had a very outgoing disposition. He didn't seem to be concerned about my presence, rather he seemed to be sizing me up. We exchanged looks back and forth for several minutes, me tipping my head one way and the eagle mirroring back to me. I almost felt like I was on trial waiting for a verdict to be rendered! Ultimately the eagle turned his back to me, apparently having made his decision. It was a very interesting encounter with a hilarious character.

"STRENGTH AND HONOUR"
Homer, Alaska

Bald eagles mate for life and these two were likely a breeding pair. This photograph was taken near Homer where their diet was being supplemented by a woman named Jean Keene. For decades Jean would put out fish scraps for the eagles that would come to her yard, helping them back from the brink of extinction. Bald eagles reach maturity between four and five years of age at which point the feathers on their head moult from brown to the more distinctive white. They are a truly regal bird and it is wonderful to get to watch them interact with one another.

RESPECT NATURE RESPECT NATURE RESPECT NATURE RESPECT NATURE

"FAMILY TIME"
Prince Albert National Park, Saskatchewan
(left)

Every spring mated pairs of Canadian geese nest along the shores of the Waskesiu River. The goslings seen here would have been a few days old as they played in the ripples in the river alongside their parents. They are very fast little swimmers and seemed to enjoy the ripples of the river on this particular evening. Canadian geese typically have between five and seven chicks a season and the young will remain with their parents for up to a full year.

The family heading down the Waskesiu River.

A blue-winged teal taking a bath in the Waskesiu River.

TURE RESPECT NATURE RESPECT NATURE RESPECT NATURE RESPECT NATURE

Sunsets are short-lived, but not for the one who lives them.

Jason Leo Bantle

"EVENING REPOSE"
Homer, Alaska

This photograph was taken near Jean Keene's eagle sanctuary in Homer. In late winter the eagles pass through on their way to summer nesting grounds. There is often low cloud in the evenings there and vibrant sunsets are not common. As a result, I was excited to have a subject matter such as this perched eagle when a beautiful sunset did present itself. The colour of the sky that evening was fantastic. I had to be careful to not stare at the sun too long as a camera lens does not provide any protection from the harmful rays.

Jason Leo Bantle

SUNSET marks the end of a day in the field. A breathtaking sunset is often a bit easier to predict than a sunrise. As the day begins to draw to a close, cloud formations and weather conditions can be evaluated and an educated guess can be made as to whether the sky will cooperate or not. In the end though, it is still up to Mother Nature and sometimes a sky that seemed to have little colour potential will reveal something spectacular. Atmospheric particles can affect the intensity of a sunset. Things such as smoke from forest fires or grain dust over the prairies act as natural filters and can increase the depth of the colour. The opportunity to photograph a sunset is short-lived so it is important to choose a desirable backdrop ahead of time. Getting prepared ahead of time is the trick to photographing sunsets.

SUNRISE happens at the start of the day and depending on the time of the year and your location, this can mean a very early start or a very late night! There is often no way to predict what first light will bring, Mother Nature has seemingly endless colour choices at her disposal. The colours of a sunrise are typically the richest in the minutes before the sun comes up on the horizon. The colours evolve and change quickly and the whole event often lasts only ten minutes or so. This does not leave a photographer much time to identify potential in the sky, find a location, get set up and get the shot before the moment has passed. A beautiful sunrise is most effective when there is a frame of reference and typically a backlit landscape is ideal for this purpose. A slight underexposure with film designed to capture depth of colour, such as Velvia, is required to do justice to this type of scene. Scouting potential sites in advance and being up early and in position ahead of time is crucial for photographing sunrises.

EVENING SKIES are captured from sunset to sunrise. The opportunities for photography at night include things like spectacular electrical storms and dancing aurora borealis. Lightning storms can be exciting but also dangerous to capture on film. To avoid a close call it is important to stay under cover. Lightning shots are captured with a camera on a tripod and a long exposure. A spot is chosen, the camera is set in position and then Mother Nature has to cooperate and place the lightning in the shot. Occasionally there will be a second strike in almost the same spot and by using a long exposure both strikes can be captured in the same image. Northern lights occur on calm, clear nights in the northern regions of Canada. They are the result of collisions between gaseous particles in the Earth's atmosphere with charged particles released from the sun's atmosphere. As with lightning work, a tripod and a long exposure are used to capture northern lights. The aurora must dance in the sky in a distinctive line in order for the film to be properly exposed. The colours can vary and using a film designed to capture depth of colour is necessary. Staying out well past dark is vital to photograph evening skies.

Sunset, Sunrise and Evening Skies

Jason Leo Bantle   47

"SUNRISE AT SPRUCE RIVER"
Prince Albert National Park, Saskatchewan
(above)

It's no secret to those that know me that I'm not an early riser by nature. That said, when I am working on a specific project I am often up well before the sun. The project on this particular morning was river otters. For over a month, I would get up very early and head to the Narrows in Prince Albert National Park to try to be in position before the otters got up for the day. I have found many times in my career that often the best shot is the one that I wasn't expecting. The otters weren't cooperative but one beautiful winter morning I witnessed this sunrise over the Spruce River. The sky started a deep red and then evolved to a vibrant orange as the sun appeared over the horizon. It was exceptional and made the early morning well worth it!

The ruffed grouse commonly seen in Prince Albert National Park.

"STRIKE"
Tweedsmuir, Saskatchewan

When I saw a summer storm approaching one evening, I grabbed my camera gear and drove to a spot near my home where I hoped to capture it. There is something to be said about the power of a thunderstorm and after a few close calls in the past I now always remain in my vehicle when photographing them. This storm passed quickly but I was able to get a shot of the lightning strike and the purple sky that it created. Actually, it probably struck very near my house. There is a certain amount of luck required when photographing lightning, a tripod and a long exposure are fundamental but beyond that it's up to Mother Nature to cooperate.

RESPECT NATURE RESPECT NATURE RESPECT NATURE RESPECT NATURE RESP

"NORTHERN ILLUMINATION"
Besnard Lake, Saskatchewan

A beautiful, clear fall evening allowed for this photograph of the aurora borealis and the nearly full moon. If you look closely you can see a number of different constellations. This area of northern Saskatchewan is very special to me and I have had great luck when it comes to photographing northern lights there. This night was exceptional as the green lights danced across the sky above me.

Jason Leo Bantle   51

"MOUNTAIN EVENING"
Banff National Park, Alberta

On a beautiful evening in the mountains the sky seemed to come alive over the Fairholme Range. There's no way to plan for a sky like this, all you can do is hope that you're ready to capture it when it presents itself. This photograph has not been filtered or enhanced in any way, the colours were simply incredible that evening. It was a great finish to a day in the field.

"PRAIRIE DAY"
Rosetown, Saskatchewan
(right)

For many, a rich blue sky dotted with fluffy white clouds and a yellow canola field below is what the prairies are all about. On this day the scene couldn't have been more perfect, complete with two old farm buildings on the horizon line! I felt fortunate to have come upon the ideal scene to represent the spirit of the prairies that day!

Thousands of tired, nerve-shaken, over-civilized people, are beginning to find out that going to the mountain is going home; that wildness is necessity; that mountain parks and reservations are useful not only as fountains of timber and irrigating rivers, but as fountains of life.

John Muir

Mountain scenes from the Bow Valley.

Jason Leo Bantle   57

RESPECT NATURE RESPECT NATURE RESPECT NATURE RESPECT NATURE RESP

"LASTING LEGACY"
Karrak Lake, Nunavut

The Inuksuk is a symbol synonymous with the Inuit people of Canada's Arctic. The name means 'something which acts for or performs the function of a person'. These man-made landmarks scatter the barrenlands and have been used historically for everything from markers for hunting grounds to reference points for navigation. This was a beautiful Arctic evening in late May. At this time of year the sun goes below the horizon for just a few hours before rising again. The setting sun created a halo effect behind the Inuksuk, which proved to be a simple yet effective subject matter.

"SUNDOGS"
Prince Albert National Park, Saskatchewan
(right)

This image was taken during the same January week that "Road Warriors" was captured. It was a crisp morning to say the least, the truck thermometer wouldn't even register the temperature it was so cold! On winter days when the air is filled with ice crystals, patches of light known as sundogs can often be seen on either side of the sun. They are refractions of the sun's rays and usually look like small rainbow-coloured patches hanging in the sky. The bitterly cold day created this beautiful scene, fresh snow on a frozen lake and sundogs in the sky above.

Sundogs on the prairies.

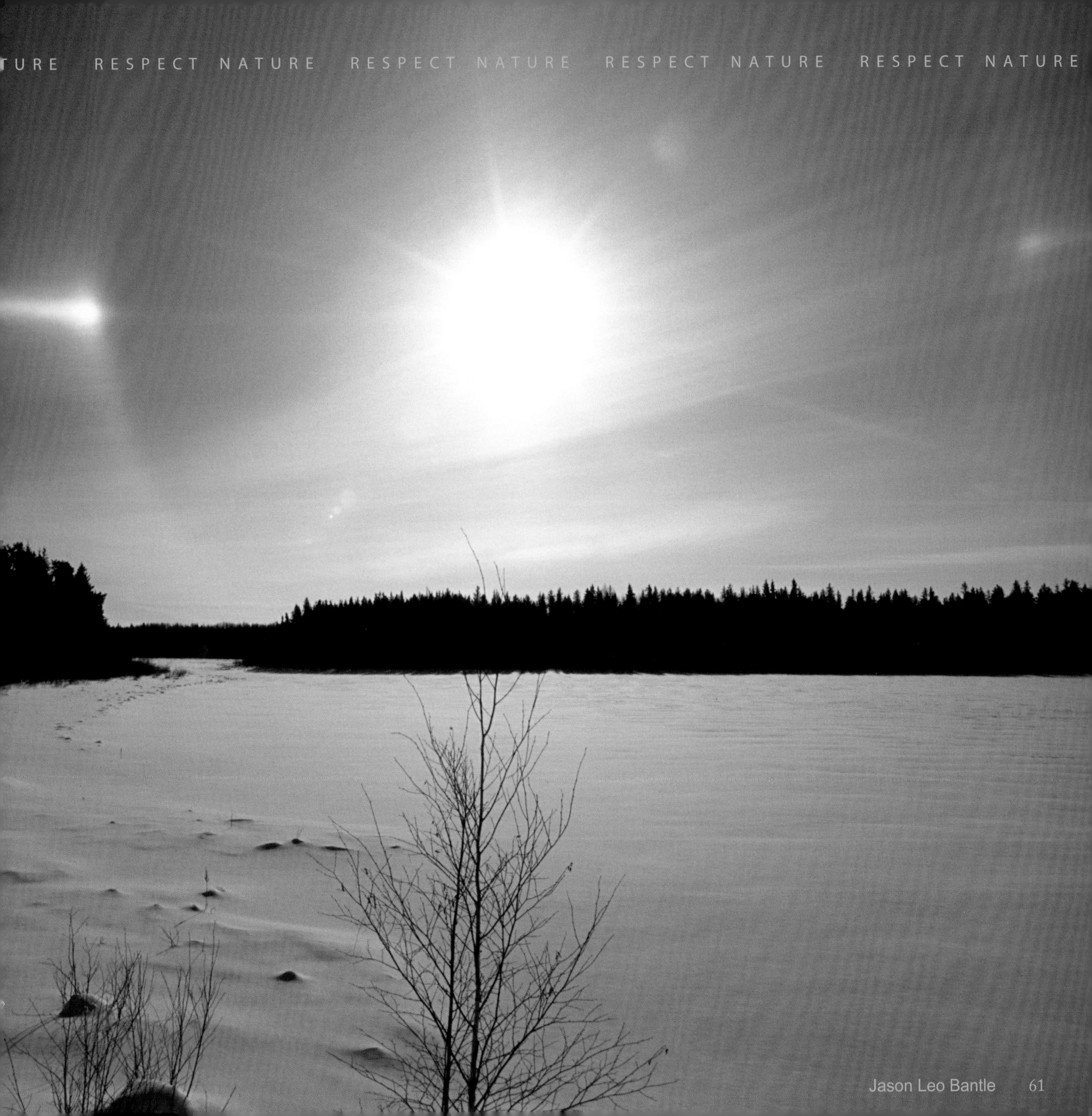

"VERMILION LAKES CALM"
Banff National Park, Alberta

The Vermilion Lakes are a series of three picturesque lakes located just outside of the Banff townsite. What makes these bodies of water so visually appealing is that quite often mountains such as Rundle, seen in this image, are reflected in the calm surface of the water. The light this particular evening was very soft and gave the scene a water-coloured effect.

Jason Leo Bantle   63

Ice and snow of the Rockies.

RESPECT NATURE RESPECT NATURE RESPECT NATURE RESPECT NATURE RESP

"NATURE'S CANVAS"
Waterton Lakes National Park, Alberta

One September I was in Waterton to photograph black bears as they fed on berries before winter. A gorgeous sunset always feels like a bonus at the end of a day in the field and this one was exceptional. I've often thought of the sky as Mother Nature's canvas, where she can paint with the most vibrant of colours. On this evening, the colours changed steadily over several minutes allowing me to capture the mountains in silhouette as the

"CREATIVE EARTH"
Emma/Christopher Lakes, Saskatchewan

Technically speaking this photograph was a challenge to capture. I set my camera on my tripod and then used a long exposure while I panned the camera vertically. The result was an abstract image of a stand of aspen trees. The beautiful fall colours combined with the white lines of the trees draw the viewer in and allow them to get lost in the serenity of the image. These aspen trees are part of a forest that provides a crucial habitat for many creatures and is a place where I love to spend time.

The same aspen forest without any creative photography.

Go out and enjoy the trees, and not just in newsprint.

Another strike captured that evening.

"THE RUNDLE RIDGE RUMBLE"
Canmore, Alberta
(right)

Summer storms in the mountains can be quite dramatic. This image was taken in late May when the Bow Valley experienced a storm that lasted several hours. You could almost feel the electricity in the air as I waited for the storm to reach the spot over Rundle Ridge where I hoped to capture it. I watched and photographed this incredible storm until well after midnight. The thunder rumbling in the background provided the soundtrack for the night.

GRIZZLY BEARS are most commonly found throughout western and northern Canada as well as in Alaska. The distinctive hump over their shoulders is a muscle mass that powers their forelimbs for digging. The grizzly bear is omnivorous, their diet consists of everything from berries to salmon to rodents depending on the region where they live. In the springtime they can often be found in open meadows feeding on rich, succulent vegetation. This time of year offers many opportunities for photographing grizzlies as they tend to be in well lit, open areas. As fall approaches and the bears begin to prepare for winter, their dietary choices switch to berries and, in coastal areas, spawning salmon. The challenge during this time of year is that the bears are often so busy eating that they refuse to look up for the camera! The bears may be easier to find in the fall, but the conditions are often more challenging for photography than they are at other times. Thick berry bushes and dark river shorelines create low-light conditions which forces a photographer to use slower shutter speeds. Being prepared for the moment that the subject chooses to cooperate is critical when photographing grizzly bears.

BLACK BEARS are found throughout most of Canada and much of North America. They are equally well-adapted to live in boreal forests and coastal areas, in parkland regions and alpine terrains. They are smaller than a grizzly bear and are far more common. The global population is estimated to be twice that of all other bear species combined. These bears can range in colour from black to brown to the nearly white subspecies known as the Kermode bear. Like the grizzly, they are omnivores that rely heavily on vegetation in their diet. In the spring they too can be found grazing in open meadows. As a wildlife photographer it can be exciting to find a mother black bear with cubs as the cubs are quick to scramble up a tree when startled. This trait can provide excellent opportunities for photography. As summer turns to fall, black bears will spend their time feeding heavily on berries. With their dark fur, contrast and lighting are frequently issues when it comes to capturing black bears on film. They are constantly moving and slow shutter speeds mean that often images are too blurred to be useable. Needing the right lighting conditions is a reality when photographing black bears.

POLAR BEARS are found in the polar regions of Canada and elsewhere within the Arctic Circle. They are typically spotted along coastlines or out on the sea ice. Although appearing to be white, a polar bear's fur is actually translucent and hollow with black skin below. These hollow tubes allow sunlight to be drawn directly to the skin which helps to keep the bears warm. Polar bears are carnivorous with the ringed seal forming the majority of their diet. Although they are excellent swimmers, polar bears cannot out-swim a seal in the water. Instead, they will wait at breathing holes and strike when a seal comes up for air. Churchill, Manitoba is known as the polar bear capital of the world. In the fall bears will congregate along the Churchill coast and wait for the sea ice to form so that they can go hunting. This is a common place to photograph polar bears as they favour the area. The sea ice forms here first and generation after generation of polar bears have passed this knowledge down to their young. In order to photograph polar bear cubs one must venture out in February or March. This is the time when mother bears are traveling with their young cubs from their den site towards the coast. The cubs have to stop often to rest and this can provide a photographer with incredible events to capture. When polar bears are active the lighting conditions are generally good but the cold can wreak havoc on equipment. Film becomes brittle and battery life is greatly reduced under these frozen circumstances. Enduring the cold can be one of the challenges of photographing polar bears.

Grizzly, Black and Polar Bears

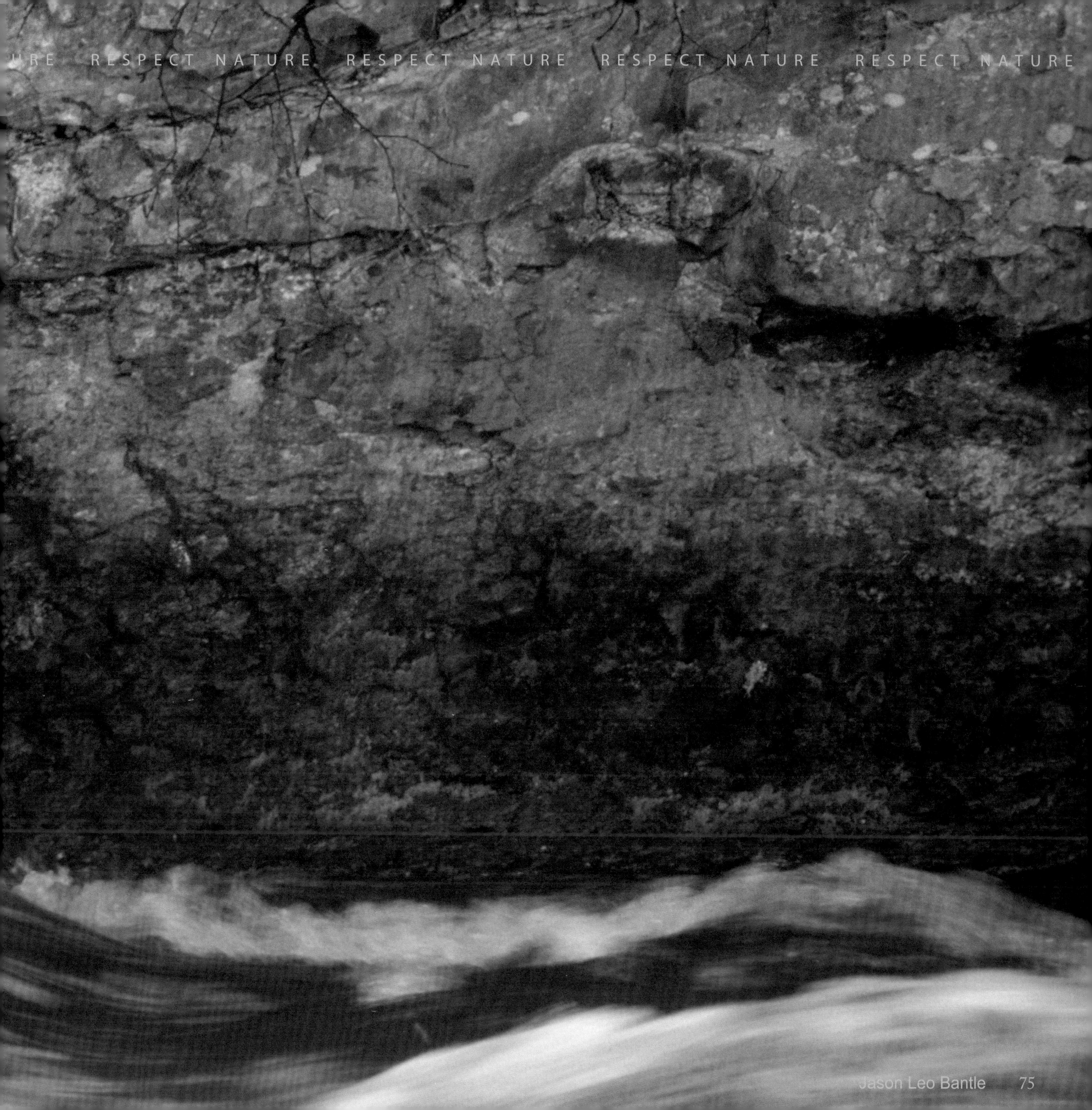

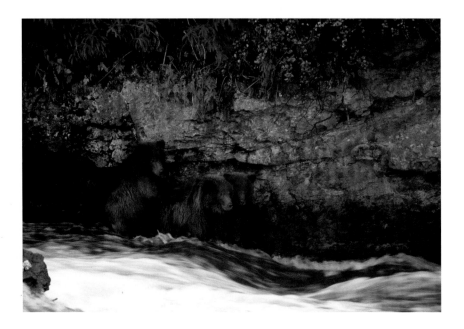

"WADING POOL"
Katmai National Park, Alaska
(above)

Katmai National Park is one of my favourite places to photograph grizzly bears. Salmon play an important role in the diet of these bears and they are plentiful in this area. The mother to the three cubs in this photograph had crossed the river to fish. The river was flowing too quickly for the triplets to follow so they anxiously waited for her to return. The cubs were also keenly aware of the presence of a large male bear that was slowly making his way towards them. I photographed the cubs as they jostled for position so as not to be the first to meet the male bear. Of course, mother bear was also watching the situation closely and she soon returned to her cubs. Once reunited, the family headed off into the woods together.

Mother grizzly fishing across the river.

"GENTLE SOUL"
Canadian Rockies

This image was captured while I was in a zodiac boat at the mouth of the Khutzeymateen River. The grizzly in this shot was feeding on grasses and sedges along the shore, very near the edge of the water. We drifted slowly in the zodiac until we were only about twenty meters away. The bear was certainly aware of our presence but had a very gentle demeanour and didn't appear to be concerned. Typically this isn't the kind of situation that I would enter into with a full grown grizzly, but the circumstances were such that I wasn't overly worried. When the bear lifted his head from his grazing I captured this photograph. Grasses in front of his face created a diffused effect.

What we saw on the first few days of our spirit bear search.

"LEGEND OF THE RAINFOREST"
Princess Royal Island, British Columbia

The spirit, or Kermode, bear is a rare and elusive creature.   Recessive genetic traits for coat colour result in about ten percent of the local black bear population being born with white or cream-coloured coats in this area. I had spent many days at this point on an excursion to try to find the legendary spirit bear. Two other photographers and I were starting to lose hope when a report came in that one had been spotted fishing in a nearby creek. We were truly fortunate to get the chance to see this individual, one of an estimated four hundred in the world!

The legend of the Gitg'at and Kitasoo Aboriginal peoples tells that when the glaciers of the Ice Age receded Raven made everything green. He decided to make one in ten black bears white, to remind him of the time when the world was white with ice and snow. Raven set aside an island paradise for these bears known as Princess Royal Island. According to the legend these bears will never leave the island; it is a remote paradise.

"IN LOVE"
Canadian Rockies

These two grizzly bears were in the midst of the mating season. With grizzlies the males court the females by following them and vocalizing. The courtship can take several days until the male gains the female's trust and has successfully defended his mate from other sires. Once the courtship period is over, the mating period will begin. This usually takes place over several more days. The large male in this photograph had a scar on his head, probably the result of a fight over this female. The interaction between these two bears was intense and at times the male would look over in our general direction. When that happened I couldn't help but feel a little anxious, like we were interrupting something despite the fifty yards of water between us.

Photographs of the large dominant male of the area.

The male courting the female.

"MOM AND HER GANG"
Churchill, Manitoba
(left)

This image is of the same polar bear family seen in my photograph entitled "Stickin' with Mom". While traveling from the den site to the Hudson Bay to hunt seals the family stopped for a break. The triplets nursed and played and were having a rest with mom at this point. Their muscles are not yet fully developed so the cubs can only travel so far before they begin to tire and require a rest. This mom was patient with her rambunctious cubs and we watched them for the better part of an afternoon before they headed off again. Triplets are not common and I felt fortunate to have the chance to photograph this thriving, healthy family.

"TREKKING IN THE ROCKIES"
Jasper National Park, Alberta
(above)

I first spotted these black bear cubs feeding with their mother along the Icefields Parkway in Jasper National Park. The mother was quite shy and moved the cubs deeper into the forest when several other vehicles stopped to watch them. I was confident that when the road got quiet again the bears would return to feed on the new green grass in the ditch so I waited quietly. My prediction was correct and shortly thereafter the family returned. I got to spend close to twenty minutes alone with the bears while mom grazed and the cubs scampered along behind her.

"FRIENDLY SPIRIT"

Princess Royal Island, British Columbia
(right)

Spirit bears exist in many areas of coastal British Columbia, but the majority of these genetically-unique black bears live on Princess Royal Island. While on this spirit bear excursion I was lucky to befriend our Aboriginal guide. He was more than willing to share his knowledge of these bears, as well as some of the native legends about them. He told me that the people of the area feel that the white-coloured bears have a calmer and more docile demeanour than their black counterparts. He told me one traditional story of a spirit bear visiting his community of Klemtu. An elder went out to meet the bear and welcomed it, asking it to be friendly during its stay. The bear agreed and the community experienced no problems during the weeks it was there! It was nice to hear a story where bears are accepted in this way as opposed to being feared and chased away by people.

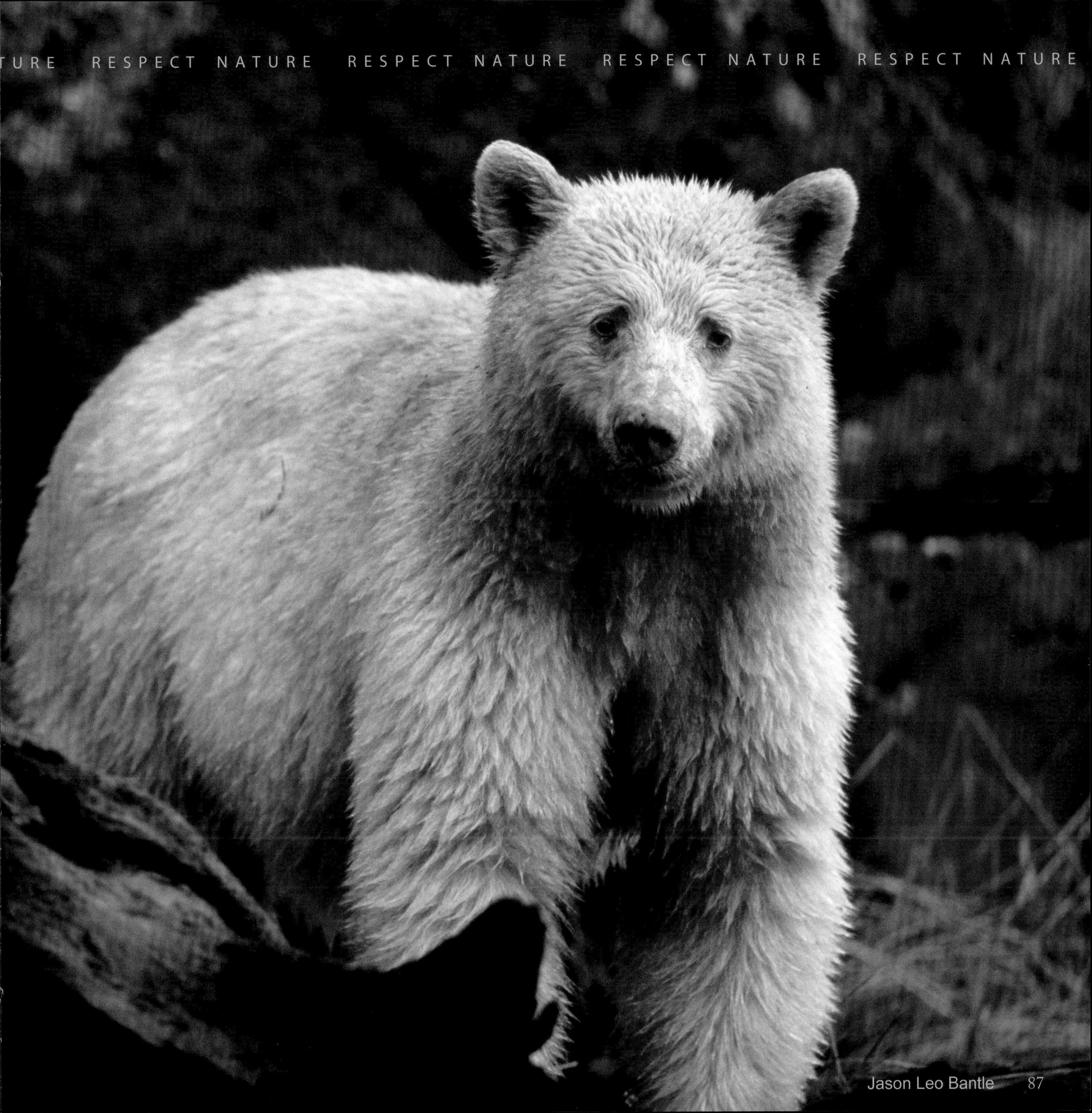

Jason Leo Bantle

Friendly Spirit heading back upstream.

Jason Leo Bantle   89

"BEACHCOMBER"
Canadian Rockies

On the coast of British Columbia lies an area known as the Khutzeymateen. This special spot is home to around fifty grizzly bears and is a sanctuary with no hunting and limited human access. This blonde-coloured grizzly was searching the coast for food at low tide. He looked under rocks and dug in the mud searching for nutrient-rich shellfish. He was especially good at opening mussel shells with his long claws. It is amazing to see how dexterous the paws of these large animals can be!

Beachcomber digging for mussels.

Beachcomber tasting the air.

The Khutzeymateen Valley.

"MOMMA BEAR"
Prince Albert National Park, Saskatchewan
(left)

One spring day while out scouting the woods for wildlife, I happened to spot a little black bear cub up in a tree. Then, suddenly, two more cubs appeared! They were triplets, two black cubs and one with a brown coat. The situation was not ideal as the mother bear had to be nearby. I grabbed my camera and was snapping some shots of the cubs when the mother bear presented herself. She was a big, healthy female and I quickly captured a few shots of her before exiting the area.

"FINDING BALANCE"
Knight Inlet, British Columbia

This image was photographed a number of years ago. Five different images from this nineteen-shot series were included in my first coffee table book and were entitled "Out on a Limb". Another photographer and I were out and witnessed this grizzly bear walk along a fallen log, get to the end and jump off into the river! It wasn't until after the event occurred that I was informed that the other photographer had run out of film and I was the only one to capture it! With the early morning light the bear is beautifully backlit as he searches the river for salmon. At a time when so many of us are working to find balance in our lives, this grizzly managed to find it in the most literal sense!

"RIDING BEARBACK"
Churchill, Manitoba

This mother polar bear had been taking a rest with her two cubs as they traveled towards the coast near Churchill. The cubs had taken the opportunity to sleep, eat and play, and had been quite entertaining to watch and photograph. Finally, mom seemed to feel that is was time to move on. She spent a few minutes rolling in the snow alongside the cubs, possibly signaling to them that something was about to happen. One of the cubs scrambled up onto her back as if to protest the fact that it was time to start walking again. Perhaps the little one wasn't ready to keep walking yet and thought that he would ride on mom instead!

"STICKIN' WITH MOM"
Churchill, Manitoba
(above)

This mother polar bear was en route to the Hudson Bay with her cubs to hunt seals. Her triplets would have been about two months old at this point, finally big enough to make the long trek to the coast. It is a crucial trip for mom; she hasn't eaten in over eight months and is in dire need of a meal. Due to her hunger, mom would try to keep the cubs moving along, but at times they simply refused because they needed a rest. When this happened mom would stop for a break to nurse the cubs and let them rest and play. In order to photograph this scene I traveled out with local Aboriginal people in snow track vehicles. By law, we were not permitted to approach closer than one hundred meters. Despite our respectful distance the cubs were shy of what we were up to and stuck close to mom. After a short break the family continued on their trek.

Mom and her cubs heading off again on their trek to the coast.

Jason Leo Bantle   95

RESPECT NATURE RESPECT NATURE RESPECT NATURE RESPECT NATURE RESP

"MOUNTAIN GRIZZ"
Jasper National Park, Alberta

At first I spotted this female grizzly feeding with her two cubs quite a distance away. I watched to see what direction they were heading and then moved into a position that I felt would be close enough for a photograph but far enough away to stay safe. I was with a few other people, this is not the kind of situation that I would have entered into had I been alone. Ultimately, the sow crested the ridge and I captured this frame. As winter approaches grizzlies can eat up to two hundred thousand berries a day to prepare for hibernation. They have to cover a lot of ground in the day to do this so I decided not to stay in the area more than a few minutes, not wanting to suddenly find myself in their desired path. We cautiously headed in the other direction, leaving the family completely undisturbed.

A spirit bear searching and lunging for salmon in the river.

"CATCH AND RELEASE"
Princess Royal Island, British Columbia
(opposite page, top)

On three consecutive days I was fortunate to get to watch this spirit bear as it fished for salmon. When it wasn't raining, the bear had the luxury of being a picky eater. Although he had no problem catching the pink salmon in the river, the larger and less common chum salmon were his preference. When he caught a chum he would head back into the forest to eat before returning for another. When he caught a pink salmon often he would determine that it wasn't what he wanted and would release it back into the river. It was a very interesting behaviour to witness and I was excited to see that I had captured both the bear and the freed fish in this shot!

Standing beside the river where
we found this spirit bear.

"PROCEED WITH CAUTION"
Coastal British Columbia
(above)

This mother grizzly bear was out fishing in the rain with her cub. The cub would likely be referred to by researchers as a "COY" which stands for "cub of the year". The mother was aware of our presence and, although we were careful to maintain a safe and respectful distance, she seemed to be uncomfortable. She positioned herself between us and her cub as if to tell us that we were close enough. This area of coastal British Columbia is known for its high concentration of grizzly bears. They take full advantage of the excellent access to salmon spawning in the rivers. On one occasion we witnessed this mother bear chase away another grizzly that had gotten too close to her cub.

Two other visitors to the river.

"LURE OF THE ROCKIES"
Canadian Rockies
(top)

It is quite common to see bears stand on their hind legs to investigate sights and smells. It is likely that this individual had caught wind of another grizzly in the area and was trying to spot it in the distance. I took advantage of the opportunity to capture the bear looking towards the mountains in the distance. It seems that perhaps humans aren't the only species to feel the lure of the Rockies!

"THE WANDERER"
Churchill, Manitoba

There was something almost haunting about the sight of a lone polar bear making his way across this vast frozen setting. The fact that the ice on this pond was thick enough to hold the bear's weight is an indicator that the sea ice would soon be able to support him as well. The ice along the coast of the Hudson Bay near Churchill is some of the first to freeze over in the fall. The reason being the fresh water flowing out of the Churchill River freezes before salt water. The prevailing wind blows this ice against the coast near Churchill which draws many polar bears to its edges. Polar bears have no distinct home range and instead spend their time wandering in search of their diet staple, the ringed seal.

Cold, inhospitable and billions of blackflies, ahh the Arctic!

"BLACK BEARY BUSH"
Prince Albert National Park, Saskatchewan
(left)

This black bear was enjoying a meal of berries near the Heart Lakes in Prince Albert National Park. It was a memorable individual and I had seen her on a couple of other occasions in the same area. Once, earlier in the year, there was a large male following her and I concluded then that this was a female. This made me optimistic that I would see her with cubs the following year. In the fall berries make up a large portion of a black bear's diet and they will spend most of their day going from bush to bush. This bear was so focused on eating that it was difficult to get her photograph, there always seemed to be branches blocking her face!

"BALANCING ACT"
Princess Royal Island, British Columbia
(far right)

This spirit bear came down to the river about
every half hour to fish. He would catch a
fish and then take it back up to the forest
to eat it before returning for another. This
particular year the salmon numbers were
good but the year before that hadn't been
the case. Our Aboriginal guides told us that
they had found a number of bears the previ-
ous spring that had perished in their dens
over the winter. This was likely due to being
in poor condition from lack of nourishment
before going into hibernation. There is most
definitely a balancing act in nature and in
this case, the forests, rivers, salmon and bears
are inextricably linked.

"STANDING IN PARADISE"
Canadian Rockies

I often find that I get an idea of what I'd like a scene to look like and then I go about trying to find something that matches that vision. I can remember seeing the lupines in bloom in this area and thinking how great it would be to come across a grizzly in a field full of them. I could hardly believe my luck when I not only found this grizzly in a lush field dotted with the purple lupines but when he cooperated by standing up to look around. This was a young male grizzly who was probably keeping an eye out for larger, more dominate males as it was mating season in the Khutzeymateen Valley. This area of the British Columbia coast is literally a grizzly's paradise.

Man's heart away from Nature becomes hard.
Standing Bear

Standing in Paradise hidden behind a tree.

Lupines partially submerged at high tide.

RESPECT NATURE   RESPECT NATURE   RESPECT NATURE   RESPECT NATURE   RESP

ARCTIC UNGULATES include barren-ground caribou and musk ox. Caribou tend to be quite curious and trusting animals. It is possible that a strong herd instinct causes caribou to be drawn towards other creatures, even a human photographer if they don't feel threatened. These traits mean that it is not uncommon to have a caribou walk right up and it is often possible to work in close proximity to them. By contrast, musk ox are quite shy and are easily alarmed. They are inclined to avoid any disturbance caused by the presence of humans. They are constantly on the lookout for anything suspicious and are quick to leave an area if they are the slightest bit uncomfortable. A slow approach is the only way to get close enough to photograph musk ox without scaring them away. Staying low to the ground by belly-crawling among rocks or peeking over the crest of a hill are tactics that can be successful. Knowledge of the subject is beneficial when photographing arctic ungulates.

MOUNTAIN UNGULATES include animals such as bighorn sheep and mountain goats. Moose prefer to spend their time near riverbeds and marshes where aquatic plants are plentiful. Mountain goats spend most of their time precariously perched on high rock ledges. In order to photograph them, climbing up high ridges to get close to their level is required. Species such as elk are very active during the fall rut season and give dramatic visual displays punctuated with their familiar bugle. This group of animals is often taken for granted as they seem safe compared to predatory species. That said, during the rut season male mating behaviour can create very dangerous situations and it is important to photograph them from a safe and respectful distance. Using a cautious approach is practical when photographing mountain ungulates.

PRAIRIE UNGULATES are animals such as bison and whitetail deer. They prefer to make their home on the open prairies. A good set of binoculars is helpful in finding these creatures in the distance. A slow, often camouflaged approach can then be attempted in order to get close enough to photograph them. Many prairie ungulates are hunted by humans and therefore they tend to be a very wary group. Using a blind to hide and wait near trails or watering holes can be an efficient way of capturing these individuals on film. Bison should never be approached on foot due to their size and their willingness to charge and working from the safety of a vehicle is preferable. This group is most active in the early morning and late evening when the light can be quite warm, creating wonderful opportunities for photography. Persistence is often needed when photographing prairie ungulates.

Arctic, Mountain and Prairie Ungulates

Jason Leo Bantle   113

"THE BOYS CLUB"
Banff National Park, Alberta
(above)

These three male bighorn sheep had congregated with several other bighorn sheep. It was not yet the heart of the rut season so their displays of dominance were somewhat muted. I watched as they took turns challenging one another. They would rock their weight back and then charge forward, crashing their horns together. Then those two would rejoin the group and two others would take a turn. There were no females around and it appeared that these males were simply practicing for later in the mating season.

A male antelope resting on the prairies.

"STAMPEDE"
Karrak Lake, Nunavut
(above)

The Canadian Arctic is home to some of the most uniquely cold-adapted species in the world and the prehistoric-looking musk ox is no exception. I snuck up onto a ridge in the hopes of capturing some images of this musk ox herd. In my experience they tend to be quite a skittish species and will often stampede when nervous or startled. I watched them for awhile before one of the large bulls seemed to suspect something. I was well-hidden but a shift in the wind could have easily given me away. As the herd stampeded past, the contrast of their dark bodies against the white snow provided a unique photography challenge. It is difficult to calculate the correct exposure in these types of situations but I was pleased with the end result.

Spirit of the Omingmuk

You are the spirit of the Omingmuk
Young one please understand
A legacy tested to stand
On these, the harsh barrenland.

Our ways proven strong
Even though at times they seem wrong.
You are a sacrifice
We so dearly know your price.

Young one please understand
You were missed before you were gone.
Your spirit will always stand
With us here, on the barrenland.

Jason Leo Bantle

"SPIRIT OF THE OMINGMUK"
Karrak, Nunavut

This musk ox calf was unfortunately separated from the rest of its herd. It had been a stormy few days in the Arctic and sadly it's not unusual for young calves to get separated from their herd. I was out working on arctic fox photography in a small tent for camouflage when the youngster wandered up to me. I searched the horizon in all directions with my binoculars hoping to spot the herd, but to no avail. I was able to spend several hours with the calf that afternoon which was a truly special experience. It was a tough situation for me as a biologist and wildlife photographer but I was helpless to do anything for him. When I headed back to camp, I took his image with me and wrote a poem based on the experience. Sometimes nature's ways can seem harsh and are hard for us to understand.

"AUTUMN STROLL"
Elk Island National Park, Alberta

Beautiful fall evening light cast this bull elk in silhouette as he crested a hill. The rut season had not yet begun and the elk in the area were not bugling or challenging each other. As a result, I felt safe to move into the necessary position to capture this image. Male ungulates are at their most dangerous during the fall rut season and must be respected and given space.

"PRAIRIE PIONEER"
Waterton Lakes National Park, Alberta
(above)

The bison is the largest land animal still living in North America. Small herds like this one always make me wonder what it would have been like to see these animals roaming free when their numbers were abundant. Despite being hunted nearly to extinction, the bison population is again on the rise. Wild herds are being re-introduced in many areas of the country and it is possible that the day will come that these pioneers return home once again.

"ARCTIC JOKERS"
Karrak Lake, Nunavut

These barren ground caribou were behaving like a group of jokers as they approached. Despite the fact that I was hidden behind a pile of rocks, they were incredibly curious and ended up getting quite close to me. Caribou are the only member of the deer family where both males and females have antlers. The females require their antlers to help defend their calves from wolves in the spring. Therefore, the caribou with the antlers in this image is the female and the other two are males. Their trusting and easygoing disposition provided me with more than a little entertainment that day as I watched them try to determine what exactly I was!

To the complaint, "There are no people in these photographs," I respond, "There are always two people: the photographer and the viewer."

Ansel Adams

The arctic wolf is a predator of caribou.

An "ice bow" in the Arctic.

My transportation and gear for a day in the Arctic.

Mountain Majesty with Shark Mountain in the background.

Moon over the mountains.

Mountain Majesty on one of my other scouting trips.

"MOUNTAIN MAJESTY"
Kananaskis Country, Alberta

I scouted this moose for nearly two months one year as he was the biggest male that I had found in the area. On this particular evening, I found him foraging in an open meadow. I felt that it was reasonably safe to approach as it wasn't the rut season. Rutting moose have long been my nemesis; on several occasions I have had to scramble up a tree to avoid being charged! Captured with Velvia film, the background and lighting came together with the subject to create a serene image.

*We're in a giant car heading towards a brick wall and
everyone's arguing over where they are going to sit.*
David Susuzki

"A CALCULATED RISK"
Banff National Park, Alberta

It can be hard to fathom the ledges and rock faces where mountain goats are usually spotted. Although it often seems that they are precariously perched, it's important to remember that they have evolved to thrive in high altitude environments. Their feet are well-suited for climbing steep, rocky slopes, with inner pads that provide traction and cloven hooves that can be spread apart as needed. The tips of their feet also have sharp dewclaws that allow them to virtually stick to the rocks and avoid slipping. After spotting this particular goat high on a rock face, I made my way up a nearby ridge to get into position for a photograph. I watched as he carefully made his way along, grazing as he went, obviously not the least bit concerned that a predator would follow him out there! With each careful step he was calculating the risk, despite their adaptations, a wrong step could, and sometimes does, prove fatal for these creatures.

"IN HIDING"
Emma/Christopher Lakes, Saskatchewan

While out for a drive near my home, I saw this fawn and its mother cross the road. I stopped to watch them as they bounded off into an open field. A few moments later I no longer saw the fawn. It is common for a doe to leave her fawn hiding in a safe place when alarmed. The fawn will not move from its hiding spot until its mother returns. The doe may have sensed me watching, as she circled in several different directions before leaving, obviously trying to keep all attention on her. Once she had cleared the area I snuck carefully and quickly to the spot where I had last seen the fawn. It wasn't long before I found it, curled in a little ball. I stayed just long enough to capture this image before retreating to my vehicle. I was concerned for the fawn's safety and from a distant hill watched for predators through my binoculars until the mother returned. I didn't have to wait long, within a few minutes the doe collected her baby and they headed off again together.

Ladyslippers and prairie lilies in Prince Albert National Park.

CRITTERS is the name often casually assigned to a group of animals that are small and quick. In theory, everything from a raccoon to a hare to a wolverine can be considered a critter. They tend to be quick in their movements, they dart from place to place never stopping for long. As a result, a photographer must be ready in advance to capture them. Certain critters, like the arctic hare, can be quite trusting and will allow a photographer to get very close if they are quiet in their movements. Others, like the wolverine, are far shyer and require a different approach. To capture a critter on film usually the best technique is to set up a blind in an area where they frequent and then wait. Patience can be one of the biggest challenges when attempting to photograph critters.

CATS AND CANIDS include animals such as the timber wolf, arctic fox and cougar. Wolves and cougars are especially cautious and are rarely seen. Both arctic and red foxes tend to be more curious and will occasionally approach if they feel that the situation is safe. Cats and canids are all carnivores and rely heavily on their ability to find, hunt and capture prey. They are skilled at staying hidden and are stealthy in their movements. This means that often a lot of time in the field is required to find them. When a den or kill site is found, the best thing to do is set up a blind and truly become part of the environment. Sounding and smelling like nature is important to capturing these animals on film. Not being discovered is the key to photographing cats and canids.

OCEAN MAMMALS are those that have evolved to make the water their home. This group includes whales, sea lions and otters to name a few. Some ocean mammals, such as the sea otter, spend quite a bit of time on the surface of the water or hauled out onto rocks near shore. This can present a wildlife photographer with a good opportunity to capture them. Whales spend their entire lives underwater, typically only coming to the surface for a breath of air before disappearing. This means that a photographer will often get only a glimpse of one of these giants before they are gone again. Unless underwater equipment is used this type of photography often occurs at the water's surface. Typically a boat is utilized and the resulting motion and instability requires faster shutter speeds to capture an image. Timing is essential when it comes to photographing ocean mammals.

Critters, Cats/Canids and Ocean Mammals

RESPECT NATURE RESPECT NATURE RESPECT NATURE RESPECT NATURE

Jason Leo Bantle   133

"UP CLOSE"
Karrak, Nunavut
(above)

I spent many hours in the field scouting for the elusive wolverine. When I found this individual, it appeared to be eating something. I sat and watched it for a few minutes before it scurried off. There seemed to be a hole nearby where it was feeding and I was curious to see if it was perhaps a den site. I slowly made my way towards it. When I was just about there I was startled to have a second wolverine pop its head out of the hole! We seemed to have surprised each other and the wolverine quickly ran away from me and I from it! This was a bit of a relief as wolverines have the reputation of being quite aggressive. I peered down into the hole to discover that they had been feeding on a caribou carcass. The caribou must have succumbed during the winter and was then covered over with snow. The wolverines had dug down to retrieve the carcass. I couldn't believe my good luck and went about setting up a snow blind where I would be able to observe the wolverines unnoticed. Over the next several days I watched as the wolverines returned repeatedly to feed until all of the remains were gone. On several occasions they approached my blind out of curiosity and I was only a few meters from them which allowed me to capture some very tight shots. I was honoured when this image was selected as a finalist by the BBC's 2009 Wildlife Photographer of the Year competition in the Gerald Durrell Award for Endangered Species category.

Up Close cleaning his face after a meal of caribou.

Up Close and an arctic wolf cross paths with no interaction, just a mutual respect.

"LEND ME A HAND"
Tweedsmuir, Saskatchewan
(left)

My first raccoon-raising experience was with this little female that I named Squirt. When she was old enough to start exploring we would go for long walks in the woods behind my home. It was important that she spend as much time in a natural environment as possible for she was to be re-introduced to the wild at maturity. I would usually take my camera with me when we went as Squirt would often do something entertaining! I took this photograph during one of Squirt's first tree-climbing efforts. She had spotted a tree that intrigued her and had no problem climbing up. When she was ready to turn around to come down again she was a little unsure of herself. She reached a paw out in my direction looking for me to lend her a hand. I was happy to oblige. She was an amazing creature to spend time with and was ultimately, successfully, returned to the wild.

"GOT YOUR BACK"
Tweedsmuir, Saskatchewan

These are two of the three raccoons that I raised the year after raising my first orphaned raccoon Squirt. The one standing behind was named Sloppy because of her messy feeding technique. When I tried to feed her with a baby bottle she seemed to struggle. Instead of gulping the milk down, as the others would do, she would let it spill all over her fur and would then lick it up from there! The raccoon in the foreground down on all fours was named Spuz Echo. These two were both females and were released back to the wild when they were mature. The following year I was fortunate to spot one of them with her young!

"COMPANIONS"
Prince Albert National Park, Saskatchewan
(above)

One winter day while out scouting, I spotted a wolf chasing a whitetail deer across Sandy Lake. As the deer got close to shore, the wolf backed off and I realized that its companion must be waiting ahead. Sure enough, the teamwork paid off and the unsuspecting deer was quickly taken down. I snuck towards them, camouflaged under the cover of a white blind, and watched as they ate. I would howl occasionally, to see their response, and they would tuck their tails which indicated to me that they were a young pair. I stopped about seventy-five yards from the scene and captured some photographs. The wolves were hungry and had to keep chasing away the ravens that were trying to get in on the meal!

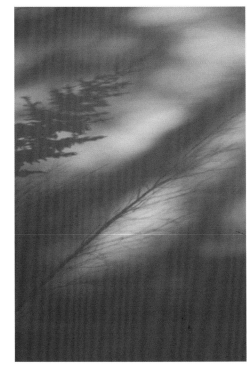

Shadows of the forest on the snow.

"ROAD WARRIORS"
Prince Albert National Park, Saskatchewan
(above)

The January day when this photograph was taken was particularly cold, the thermometer outside was reading -45°C when I headed out that morning. There had been a fresh snow-fall the night before and I wanted to use it to my advantage to look for wildlife. I made my way into Prince Albert National Park, looking for tracks. After an hour or so with no luck I was ready to head back. On the way home I crested a slight hill and discovered a pack of seven wolves resting on the road ahead of me! Animals will often travel the roadways in winter as the snow gets ploughed, making it easier to get around. The pack rose and started to trot off. I managed to get into position and capture a shot of four of the wolves; the other three had already gone into the trees. I had my winter gear with me so I quickly got organized to try to follow the pack into the forest. As soon as I got off the road though, I sunk into the hip-deep snow. I'm obviously not adapted the same way as the wolves are to travel in those types of conditions!

The same pack captured on Waskesiu Lake that year.

"A KISS FOR A PRINCE?"
Northern British Columbia

On a cool coastal morning I happened upon this western toad. He didn't seem inclined to move and I was able to creep slowly towards him and capture a close-up with my macro lens. As I looked at him I was reminded of the fairytale about the prince who was turned into a frog. I have to admit that I was glad that there was no reason for me to have to kiss this toad! Western toads are found in boreal forests throughout western North America. They are currently listed as near threatened largely due to the impact that chemical contamination is having on their environment.

"HEIR TO THE THRONE"
Off Vancouver Island, British Columbia
(above)

This sea lion was lounging on the rocks off the coast of Vancouver Island with many others. They were soaking up the warm morning sun. It is a common sight to see dozens or even hundreds of these sea mammals relaxing together on the land. This one had assumed a more regal pose than the others, almost as though he wanted to have his picture taken! Sea lions are known to be highly intelligent and are frequently trained by humans in captivity. Their ability to walk on all four flippers is what sets them apart from seals and other aquatic mammals.

"PEACEFUL POWER"

Canadian Rockies
(left)

Over the years I have had many people share their cougar experiences with me. Most of the time all you get is a fleeting glimpse; a cougar isn't usually inclined to let itself be seen. One story that I envied in particular had come from a couple who described seeing a large, tan-coloured animal walk down the middle of the road in the forest outside Banff National Park and then sit down on the road's edge. They stopped their vehicle and watched it for several minutes before it got up and headed into the trees. They weren't familiar with what the animal was but there was no doubt in my mind that they had just described my dream encounter with a cougar! A year later, my dream came true. I spent just over twenty days in the field, scouting an area known for cougars with someone with great expertise. I had almost given up hope when, on one of the final mornings of the excursion, we spotted a cougar on a ridge with binoculars. We were near the safety of a vehicle and only about eighty meters from the cat. It would prove to be a very peaceful encounter with a very powerful animal. I got to photograph it for three to five minutes before it got up and made its way towards us down the ridge and disappeared into the trees. They are well-adapted to maintain secrecy and I'm sure that I've been in the wilds other times when cougars have been around but have not shown themselves. When I got my film back I noticed the faint spotting on the cougar's hind end, indicating that it was still young, hence a little more curious. It was a rare encounter and one that I won't soon forget.

Whitetail deer are the primary prey of cougars.

"DREAMING OF SPRING

Karrak Lake, Nunavut
(left)

This female arctic fox was sleeping near her den. This image was taken in mid-May, shortly before she would have given birth to her kits. Mated pairs of arctic foxes den and raise their kits together until well after the young are weaned. The male will bring food to the den for the female after the kits are first born to help her keep her strength up. This can be a big job as the arctic fox has an average of eleven kits per litter with the largest litter on record containing an astounding twenty-two kits! I spent several days around this den site to gain the female's trust. By the time I captured this photograph she would let me get within a few feet of her. I couldn't help but wonder as I watched her sleep if she was dreaming of the spring to come.

The end of my camera lens a mere few feet from Dreaming of Spring.

"GOING WITH THE FLOW"
Near Seward, Alaska

Sea otters are such a playful species that it is great fun to photograph them. When resting, sea otters will often clasp paws with one another to keep from drifting too far out to sea. When they do the group is referred to as a raft. Typically a raft will consist of anywhere from ten to one hundred individuals but can be much larger. The largest raft ever recorded contained two thousand individual sea otters! The otters in this photograph were resting in a quiet bay and seemed to simply be floating along as they enjoyed the warm Alaskan sun.

Ocean, the rhythms of its waters are soothing!

Jason Leo Bantle

"SOUL OF THE PACIFIC"
Off Vancouver Island, British Columbia
(above)

The orca whale is synonymous with the pacific coast. We are often granted just a glimpse of these majestic creatures as they glide along below the surface. This individual came up for a breath of air just in front of the small boat that I was in. As the largest member of the dolphin family, a full grown male will measure over twenty feet in length and will often weigh around six tonnes! The water was especially clear on this day and when the whale swam under our boat it made me realize just how big he was. The orca plays a culturally significant role for the Aboriginal peoples of the area and their presence is also vital for the health of the ocean ecosystem.

"ON THE MOVE"
Karrak Lake, Nunavut

The wolverine is perhaps one of the most elusive species in North America and as a result enjoys an almost mythic reputation. I felt extremely fortunate to finally have the opportunity to capture one of these little creatures on film after many excursions to the Arctic. In fact, until the year that this photograph was taken, I was the only researcher to have been at this particular camp that hadn't seen a wolverine! This wolverine had passed by camp on several occasions and had quite a curious nature. They seem to be constantly loping. One day I decided to track him, I followed him by snowmobile for over twenty-six kilometres during which time he only stopped twice to scent mark otherwise his tracks showed him loping the entire trail. Research has shown that a wolverine can maintain a home range of several hundred square kilometers. Their life is truly one of endurance and they are perfectly adapted to the often harsh realities of their environment.

"I'M A LITTLE SHY"
Prince Albert National Park, Saskatchewan

Play is essential to the development of all young mammals. Play behaviour allows muscles to develop and triggers natural instincts. In predators such as fox kits, play behaviour will help them learn how to be good hunters. A kit will practice stalking and pouncing on its siblings long before it attempts the same manoeuvres with potential prey. This young fox was playing with its siblings close to their den site. In this image it almost looks like he's doing his stretching exercises before the big game or perhaps was just being shy! Although it is always nice to see young animals in their environments, these fox kits were especially entertaining.

Red fox kits playing and relaxing outside of their den.

A member of the pack walking in towards us.

A member of the pack walking away from us.

One of the pack members howling.

A few of the pack members investigating our snow machines.

"THE MATRIARCH"

Carrak Lake, Nunavut

One of the most incredible wolf encounters that I've had to date came barely a day into a month-long Arctic excursion. Other researchers and I were out scouting for arctic fox dens when I thought I heard something in the distance. We all listened and sure enough could hear faint howling in the distance. I scanned the horizon with my binoculars and spotted three wolves at the top of a hill in the distance. As I watched, two more crested the hill, then another group, and another. Within minutes there were seventeen wolves on the distant hillside, howling. We estimated the wolves to be about six kilometres away so decided to head for a rock outcrop that was close to our proximity. En route I noticed two wolves walking about three kilometres around us. I was disappointed, sure that we had missed our chance to be close enough for a photograph as they were headed in the wrong direction. The disappointment quickly gave way to excitement however, as suddenly two wolves came over a hill towards us. Immediately we laid down and were still. In the same instance a wolverine, the first I'd ever seen, was heading out of the area.

The two wolves circled downwind and stood about fifteen meters away, seemingly curious about us. Ultimately most of the pack took a turn coming for a smell downwind of us. They exhibited no aggression, only one raised the hairs on its back but that was likely from apprehension. It was obvious that they had recently fed and were a very healthy pack of wolves. It was a cold evening, about -25°C, and my camera batteries were weak. I kept turning my camera off to rest the batteries and would then flip it back on to get some shots. I know that there were many shots that I missed, but the excitement of the encounter was second to none. After about forty-five minutes, the wolves left the area and we headed back to camp. I grabbed some fresh batteries and then we took the snowmobile out to try to get ahead of them. We were able to get in front of them and they did approach again. The light was waning though, and this second encounter was much shorter. This image is of the alpha female who was striking not only in appearance but also in her composure and obvious ability to lead her pack.

"YOU CAN DO IT"
Kananaskis Country, Alberta

This little chipmunk was busy grooming himself in the late afternoon. I had just finished a hike in the mountains when I spotted him. They are meticulous when it comes to grooming and I thought I might be able to get an interesting shot of this behaviour. As I watched, I thought for a moment that he was about to sneeze. His body tensed and he clenched his tiny paws and shut his eyes tight. It was almost as though he was willing something to happen! I'm not sure exactly why he paused that way but the moment passed and he returned to the task at hand. These little creatures usually dart away quickly so it was nice to get a few still moments to photograph this chipmunk.

"WIDE EYED"
Lake Louise, Alberta
(above)

While out for an early evening walk I was startled by this weasel. It was running towards me on the hiking trail that runs alongside Lake Louise and had a mouse in its mouth. As it passed me I pulled my camera from my pack and, leaving my pack on the side of the trail, ran after it. When it darted into the tall grass beside the trail I was able to get into position ahead of it and wait. They are such a quick animal, rarely stopping to pose for a photograph. I stayed still when the weasel reappeared and watched where it went. When it disappeared again I quickly moved to the spot and was excited to discover a series of holes in a small slope. Adult weasels are solitary but their young are dependent on the mother for food until they are close to two months old. This weasel had indeed returned to its burrow to feed its young. I watched as little heads would pop out of the holes and then be gone again just as quickly. I was losing light when I captured this photograph and felt lucky to have discovered the family in the first place. Their eyes are large relative to their body size which inspired the title for this photograph.

"POWER STRIDE"
Canadian Rockies

After three full weeks in the field with no luck, my guide and I finally happened upon a cougar. The cougar is such a secretive animal that it probably shouldn't be a surprise to me that this was my first cougar sighting in all my years of being in the field. There are people who spend their whole lives in cougar territory and never catch more than a glimpse of one of these powerful cats. When we first spotted this cougar it was lying in the sun on a ridge. We were secure in our vehicle as we slowly approached. It didn't move right away and I was able to capture some shots of it as it lay on the ridge. A few minutes later it got up and began to walk powerfully down the ridge. It passed a cautious distance from the vehicle but my camera equipment was able to easily bridge the space between us. I couldn't have asked for a more perfect cougar encounter!

URE RESPECT NATURE RESPECT NATURE RESPECT NATURE RESPECT NATURE

An arctic hare digging through the snow to find vegetation.

An arctic hare's feet are adapted for staying above the snow.

Black tips on an arctic hare's ears attract an avian predator's attention as opposed to the whole body. It is not uncommon to see arctic hares with tears on the tips of their ears.

"A HARE WITH A PRAYER"
Karrak Lake, Nunavut
(left)

While foraging for vegetation this arctic hare would stop frequently to rub its face with its paws. I was having a good time watching as this hare would scratch at the snow with both front paws and then check to see what it had uncovered. Weighing between nine and twelve pounds on average, the main predator for the arctic hare is the arctic wolf. This individual must have sensed that I was no threat as it let me get within a few feet of it. When the film came back from this encounter I couldn't help but think that it looked like the hare was praying! In reality I had captured him as he was about to scratch his nose again.

An arctic hare uses its whiskers as sensors when digging.

"HOME SWEET HOME"
Tweedsmuir, Saskatchewan

This is a photograph of an orphaned raccoon I named Squirt. She was very young at this point, probably around four weeks old. Raccoons are born with their eyes closed and they will typically open in the third week of life. When Squirt's eyes first opened they were still slightly blue; young innocent eyes so beautiful. I made a log home for her to simulate a natural environment and she would often curl up to sleep inside of it. I guess to her it was simply home!

"THE APPLE BANDITS"
Tweedsmuir, Saskatchewan
(right)

I have been fortunate to have two separate chances to raise orphaned raccoons so far in my life. My first experience was with a single raccoon named Squirt. The following year I raised these three individuals. Two were female, Sloppy and Spuz Echo, and the third was a male named Mangler. On a beautiful fall day I took the three of them for a walk over to my neighbour's home. The crabapple tree in the yard enticed the raccoons and they quickly scrambled up. The colours were so fantastic that I ran home and returned with my camera. I was able to capture a few shots of the three of them as they played, although getting them to all look at the camera at the same instant proved to be a challenge. The next challenge came when it was time to get the little rascals to come down again; it took over an hour to convince them!

"WOLF SONG"
Prince Albert National Park, Saskatchewan
(above)

I had heard that people were seeing wolf pups in a particular area of Prince Albert National Park. I headed out to the area, stopping at various points along the road to wait, watch and listen. I've been told that if you howl wolves will sometimes howl back. After several days in the area I tried a howl in the late afternoon. To my surprise, a response came so I headed in the direction of the howling. When I arrived at the edge of a meadow I sat down and howled again. Less than twenty minutes later the wolf pup in this image and its two black siblings emerged from the trees. They sat down about twenty yards from me and we howled back and forth to one another. It was one of the most intimate experiences that I've ever had with a wolf and one that I will never forget. Over the next few days I went back many times and spotted them occasionally. One day they even happened to be on the roadway, probably trying to find a breeze to help keep the insects at bay.

Wolf Song seen in the same area during his/her first winter. *(left)*

These two black wolves were siblings of Wolf Song. *(right, right middle)*

"A KISS FOR MOM"
Prince Albert National Park, Saskatchewan

This fox kit was one of the smallest that I'd ever seen out of a den. This is a den site that is used by area foxes annually and I have had the good fortune to see many kits over the years. There were three kits in this litter and they played together at length while their mother was gone hunting. They were very excited when she returned and rushed over to give her a "welcome home" kiss! I got to see this family for several days in a row before the mother moved them. As the den becomes ridden with insects it is common for the mother to move the young to a fresh den once they are old enough.

"TERRITORIAL STAND"
Karrak Lake, Nunavut

This male arctic fox was part of an ongoing research project that I was sometimes involved with. He was nicknamed Johnny, after Johnny Cash, because of his constant vocalizations. Arctic foxes tenaciously defend their territories, however, often a vocal warning is enough to deter others from crossing the invisible borders. This fox would march up and down his territorial line with his tail in the air barking and singing the whole time, while another fox would do the same on his parallel line a little ways away. This was their way of asking each other to respect their individual space.

ACKNOWLEDGEMENTS

This book would not have been possible without the book publishing expertise and knowledge of Lori Nunn. Thanks Lori for another great team effort! I appreciate your hard work in putting my design ideas and stories into a workable format for the printing of this book. Your attention to detail, your ideas and understanding of how important respecting nature is to me is greatly appreciated. It was a pleasure to work with you Lori and thanks for all the homemade soups.

Ken Roach of Phase II Photographics in Saskatoon colour corrected all of the images you see in this book so that in book print they would look as close to the original slides as possible. Thanks Ken for m   eeting our deadlines! Also thanks for all of your expertise over the years regarding the printing and processing of my work, you are an artist!

Jeannine Douville, my sister and production manager of All in the Wild Photography, has been instrumental in the development and success of All in the Wild Photography. This book would not have been possible without the many years of your hard work, encouragement and support of your little brother! Thanks Jeannine for everything, and thank you to your family for their understanding.

Meagan Gilmour provided valuable editing comments regarding the text and layout of the book. Thanks for your support of this project, and of All in the Wild Photography; it would not be what it is today without your support, encouragement and love of nature!

To all of my family, mom, dad, Jeannine, George, Patrick and Brittney Douville, Jacqueline Bantle, Gwen, Gord, Brad, Marcia, Natalisha and Rylan Zakreski, Myles, Christopher and Amy Bantle, thank you for all of your support. I know All in the Wild Photography hasn't been the easiest road, thanks for your encouragement and help on so many occasions and in so many different ways. Love you all!

To my mom and dad, Regina and Denis, thanks for all your love and caring over the years. Mom your encouragement, love of animals and help with "business things" for All in the Wild Photography is greatly appreciated. Thanks for your encouragement and wisdom dad, for keeping my vehicles on the road so I could get my job done and your business advice!

To the people who encouraged me as a child to enjoy my love of nature, thank you Grandma Katie Bantle, Regina Bantle, Denis Bantle, Eric Eckel, Myles Bantle, and Richard Bantle. All of you taught me a lot about nature and life, your influence has carved me into the person I am today.

To all of the boys who have supported me over the years, Goose, Kimmer, Henderson, Lylee, Cory, Jeff, Fisher, Serge, and Natdog, thanks dudes!

To Elaine, your continued guidance in helping me find who I am, and what I am really about, has been instrumental in All in the Wild Photography. Thanks for all of your years of support, encouragement and caring.

To Gladys and Arnold Selander, thanks for your support and keeping my Tweedsmuir home, home and interesting!

To the following list of people and organizations that have been involved in making All in the Wild Photography and the photos in this book possible:
A. M. "Bun" Young, Jorgan Aitok, Ray Alisauskas, Dorothy Allbright, Dave Archer, Deb and Brian at the Art Preserve, Margaret and Bill Biletski, Dianne and Brian Bosomworth, Bevin Bradley, Canadian Wildlife Service (Saskatoon), Ron and Patty Cairns, Sharon and Ted Cardwell, Kim, Rebecca and John Cross, Jeff Danielson, Erin Dawson, Sheri Fisher and Mike Karras, Friesens Books, Lynn Gilmour, Carmela Giocoli, Cory Gordon, Carla and Brent Hamel, Brenna Heggie, Chris Hendrickson and Vanessa Harriman, Kathryn Hull, Jean Keena, Dana Kellett, Roland Kendal, Leagh and Don Kendal, Dick Kerbes, Ed Kirzinger, Knight Inlet Lodge, Ray Kolla, Shawn and Juanita Kolla, Serge Lariviere, Judy Lorenz, Mike Macri, Doug Neasloss, Dana Nordin, Northwest Territorial Government, Nunavut Government, Lori and Graeme Nunn, Ontario Ministry of Natural Resource, Brent Pauli, Phase II Photographics and staff, Justin Pitt, Kirk Pocha and Mary Wagner, Bob Redekopp, Karen Redeye, Ken Roach, John and Pauline Samborski, Gustaf Samelius, Lydia Schroeder, Andrea Scott, Jan and Stan Shadick, Stuart Slattery, Lawreen and Mike Spencer, Morris Spencer, Squirt, St. Peter's College, The Kids, April Tranter, University of Saskatchewan, John Waddington, Lyle, Sue, Willow and Autumn Walton, Elaine Warrington, Nathan Weibe, and to anyone I may have forgotten to mention here, thank you all!

Thanks to all of YOU who support my work!

The following photographs may be available for purchase. Please go to www.bantlephoto.com for more information. Check back often for new releases!

...continued from the introduction page 13

Well, here I am back on the train once again. This time I am headed home after an incredible experience in the wild. I find that often there is a time for reflection after a trip such as this. There is always the anticipation, and concern, as to whether or not I captured images that will do justice to my experience. One of the downsides to working with film is that I have to wait until I get home and have it processed before I know what I captured. However, the day I get the film back will be like Christmas!

More importantly, this polar bear excursion was a huge success. One of our Aboriginal guides referred to the baby polar bears we saw as "little movie stars". He couldn't have put it any better. They were ready to be famous I guess! The only worrisome thing that I am carrying at this moment is something that he said, "I have lived in Churchill for fifty-two years and I have never seen it this warm, this is nuts!" The warm weather in the north is of grave concern and I hope that the little polar bears that I have just spent time with will be able to adapt to their changing world. If they have to wait for us to make the changes that we need to, I worry that it will be too late. As the train clicks along the tracks, I feel energized from this most recent experience in the wild. I have so much to be thankful for.

Respect Nature,